IT'S MY STATE!

NEW JERSEY

David C. King

William McGeveran

 **Marshall Cavendish**
Benchmark

New York

Copyright © 2011 Marshall Cavendish Corporation

Published by Marshall Cavendish Benchmark
An imprint of Marshall Cavendish Corporation

Website: www.marshallcavendish.us

This publication represents the opinions and views of the authors based on their personal experience, knowledge, and research. The information in this book serves as a general guide only. The authors and publisher have used their best efforts in preparing this book and disclaim liability rising directly and indirectly from the use and application of this book.

Other Marshall Cavendish Offices:
Marshall Cavendish International (Asia) Private Limited, 1 New Industrial Road, Singapore 536196 •
Marshall Cavendish International (Thailand) Co Ltd. 253 Asoke, 12th Flr, Sukhumvit 21 Road, Klongtoey Nua, Wattana, Bangkok 10110, Thailand • Marshall Cavendish (Malaysia) Sdn Bhd, Times Subang, Lot 46, Subang Hi-Tech Industrial Park, Batu Tiga, 40000 Shah Alam, Selangor Darul Ehsan, Malaysia

Marshall Cavendish is a trademark of Times Publishing Limited

All websites were available and accurate when this book was sent to press.

Library of Congress Cataloging-in-Publication Data
King, David C.
        New Jersey / David C. King and William A. McGeveran, Jr. — 2nd ed.
            p. cm. — (It's my state!)
        Includes index.
        ISBN 978-1-60870-055-4
        1. New Jersey—Juvenile literature. I. McGeveran, William. II. Title.
    F134.3.K56 2011
    974.9—dc22   2010003910

Second Edition developed for Marshall Cavendish Benchmark by RJF Publishing LLC (www.RJFpublishing.com)
Series Designer, Second Edition: Tammy West/Westgraphix LLC
Editor, Second Edition: Brian Fitzgerald

All maps, illustrations, and graphics © Marshall Cavendish Corporation. Maps and artwork on pages 6, 28, 29, 75, 76, and back cover by Christopher Santoro. Map and graphics on pages 8 and 45 by Westgraphix LLC.

The photographs in this book are used by permission and through the courtesy of:
Front cover: Lisa J. Goodman/Getty Images and Sonya Etchison/Shutterstock (inset).
Alamy: Photo Network, 4 (left); Russell Kord, 10; Marc Muench, 11; Gail Mooney-Kelly, 12; Mira, 13; Tom Till, 14; Janice Hazeldine, 16; H. Mark Weidman Photography, 17; Joe Sohm/Visions of America, LLC, 22, 34; James Nesterwitz, 24; North Wind Picture Archives, 25, 26; Andrea Matone, 38; Jeff Greenberg, 40, 47; Florian Franke, 49; ClassicStock, 59; Ted Horowitz, 66; Martin Thomas Photography, 69. **AP Images:** Charles Rex Arbogast, 42; Daniel Hulshizer, 55; Mike Derer, 75. **Corbis:** 35; Kelly-Mooney Photography, 9; David H. Wells, 46; Bettmann, 48; Ed Kashi, 70. **Getty Images:** De Agostini, 4 (right); Jason Hosking, 5; James L. Amos/National Geographic, 19; Frank Lukasseck, 20 (top); Ross M. Horowitz, 20 (bottom); Jim Simmen, 21; Kean Collection/Hulton Archive, 27; Comstock Images, 31; Visions of America/Joe Sohm, 32, 56; Topical Press Agency/Stringer/Hulton Archive, 36; MPI/Stringer/Hulton Archive, 37; Jason Merritt, 51 (bottom); Dennis McColeman, 54; Jeff Zelevansky, 60; Bill Curtsinger/National Geographic, 62; Peter Anderson, 64; AFP, 65; Bruce Bennett, 71; Richard Cummins, 72 (top); Rosemary Calvert, 72 (bottom); Jonnie Miles, 73. **Library of Congress:** LC-DIG-fsa-8b27245, 50. **Shutterstock:** scoutingstock, 44; Anthony Correia, 51 (top); Kenneth Summers, 53; gary718, 61. **U.S. Fish and Wildlife Service:** 15, 18 (both).

Printed in Malaysia (T).
135642

CONTENTS

A Quick Look at
NEW JERSEY

State Flower: Purple Violet

Violets bloom across the fields and forests of New Jersey in early spring. There are more than five hundred varieties of this delicate flower, many in various shades of purple. In colonial times, violets were widely used as a food and also as a base for perfumes.

State Tree: Red Oak

The red oak is one of the best-known American hardwoods—woods that are sturdy enough for building houses and flooring. Nearly half the hardwood lumber used in New Jersey comes from its state tree.

State Bird: Eastern Goldfinch

Also known as the American goldfinch, the state bird is easy to identify because of the male's bright lemon-yellow body and black cap, wings, and tail. These birds feed on seeds from trees, shrubs, and flowers.

State Animal: Horse

The horse was a natural choice as the state animal. During the 1700s and much of the 1800s, horses were used to pull carriages, farm and freight wagons, and canal barges and boats. Before steam engines took over, horses even pulled the first railroad cars. The earliest farm machines also depended on horsepower.

State Dinosaur: Hadrosaurus

In 1858, one of the first dinosaur skeletons found in North America was unearthed in Haddonfield, New Jersey, near Camden. The skeleton belonged to a plant-eating duck-billed dinosaur called Hadrosaurus. In 1991, the state declared the Hadrosaurus its official dinosaur.

State Insect: Honey Bee

In the 1700s and early 1800s, honey was an important agricultural product in New Jersey. The fields of clover in the state's northwest corner were said to produce the best honey. Honey is still big business in the state, and it is even sold at roadside farmstands.

★ 1 ★
The Garden State

People who visit or pass through New Jersey sometimes wonder why it is called the Garden State. They often get their first glimpse of the state riding along busy stretches of the New Jersey Turnpike, past big cities such as Newark and Elizabeth. There seem to be more smokestacks than trees, more warehouses than gardens.

The confusion about the nickname is understandable. The land area of New Jersey is only 7,417 square miles (19,210 square kilometers). Only three states are smaller. Yet as of 2007, New Jersey had a population of close to 9 million people—the eleventh largest of any state. New Jersey has about 1,200 people for each square mile of land (460 per sq km), making it the most densely populated state in the country.

However, the population is concentrated in the northeast. A short drive in any direction can take you to a hilly semi-wilderness, where clear streams sparkle beneath towering oaks and maples. Not far to the south is a vast region called the Pine Barrens, where cranberry bogs give way to one of the largest forested areas on the mid-Atlantic Coast.

Quick Facts

NEW JERSEY BORDERS

North	New York
South	Delaware Bay
East	New York
	Atlantic Ocean
West	Pennsylvania
	Delaware

New Jersey has 21 counties.

New Jersey has twenty-one counties. The most crowded is Hudson County, which lies across the Hudson River from New York City. The county has more than 12,000 people per square mile (4,600 per sq km). On the other hand, Salem County, in the southwest, has only about 200 people per square mile (fewer than 80 people per sq km).

The state includes four natural land regions. The Piedmont is a belt of raised land that extends from the northeastern border with New York southwest across New Jersey. From there, the Piedmont stretches as far south as Alabama. The Highlands region of New Jersey, located northwest of the Piedmont, is a narrow strip of steep hills and valleys. In the state's far northwest corner is the Appalachian Ridge and Valley region. The bottom three-fifths of the state lies within the Atlantic Coastal Plain.

The Piedmont

In the northeast corner of New Jersey, the Hudson River separates the state from New York's Westchester County and from the towering skyscrapers of New York City. This geographic region is an area of gentle hills that is about 200 feet (60 meters) above sea level. The Piedmont covers only about one-fifth of the state's land area. But more than half the state's people live there, especially in the eastern part. Four of New Jersey's six largest cities are located in the Piedmont: Newark, Jersey City, Paterson, and Elizabeth.

One of New Jersey's many pleasant natural surprises is a region of cliffs called

The towering skyline of Manhattan is visible from just across the Hudson River in the Meadowlands of northeastern New Jersey.

the Palisades. Rising from 300 to 550 feet (90 to 170 m) above the Hudson River, these sheer cliffs extend north from Hoboken, New Jersey, to Nyack, New York, on the river's west bank. They were formed close to 200 million years ago. At the time, molten lava rose from deep in the earth's crust and hardened. Today, this dramatic wall of gray-black rock with streaks of dark red adds to the beauty of the region around the Hudson River.

Another unique feature of the Piedmont is an area called the Great Swamp National Wildlife Refuge. These wetlands were created more than ten thousand years ago, during the last Ice Age, when the movement of glaciers carved up the land. The area, within sight of New York City's skyscrapers, was at one point chosen as the site for a new airport. But New Jersey residents protested, and in 1960, the swamp was set aside as a wildlife refuge. Today, it is home to nearly one thousand plant and animal species, including more than two hundred bird species alone. Several miles of trails and boardwalks make it a user-friendly sanctuary.

The decline of manufacturing industries in recent years affected some parts of the Piedmont. For example, the Hudson River waterfront became littered with rotting piers and crumbling warehouses that had been abandoned for decades.

The rugged cliffs of the Palisades line the west bank of the Hudson River in New Jersey.

Since the late 1990s, however, the state has made efforts to repair the region. Broken-down structures have been replaced by attractive apartment complexes, row houses, and modern office buildings.

The Highlands

A short drive to the west of New Jersey's bustling cities and nearby suburbs will take travelers to the Highlands region. This is a semi-wilderness area that covers nearly 1,000 square miles (2,600 sq km) of steep hills and narrow valleys. Many of the state's eight hundred lakes and ponds are located there and provide scenic recreation areas for both residents and tourists. The Highlands region is also a vital watershed. It supplies water to millions of New Jerseyans living to the east.

The highest point in the state is located in the Kittatinny Mountains. It is marked by the High Point Monument, which was built in 1930 to honor war veterans.

The Appalachian Valley and Ridge Region

The smallest of New Jersey's land regions is located in the far northwest. The Appalachian Valley and Ridge is part of the large Appalachian Mountain chain, which stretches from the Saint Lawrence River in Canada to Georgia in the south. Part of the Appalachian Trail cuts through New Jersey in this region. The trail crosses the Kittatinny Mountains, the largest mountains in the state. The state's tallest peak reaches 1,803 feet (550 m) high. Its name is fitting: High Point.

The Delaware Water Gap, on the Delaware River, is one of New Jersey's most popular scenic areas.

The hills in this region may not be very tall, but their steepness gives them a rugged appearance. The grassy valleys and hills are perfect for apple orchards and herds of dairy cattle.

The Delaware Water Gap forms the border between northwestern New Jersey and Pennsylvania. The famous Delaware Water Gap National Recreation Area straddles about 40 miles (65 km) of the Delaware River. This is one of the most popular scenic areas in the eastern United States. It draws about 5 million visitors each year. The river is harder to get to on the New Jersey side, but there are spectacular views from Interstate 80.

The Atlantic Coastal Plain and Southern New Jersey

An invisible line runs northeast across the state, from Trenton, the state capital, to the Atlantic Coast at Perth Amboy. This is called the fall line. It is marked by waterfalls and rapids on the Raritan River and other flowing bodies of water.

The region south and east of this fall line is part of the Atlantic Coastal Plain. This region begins on Cape Cod in Massachusetts and extends down the eastern seaboard to Georgia. The Atlantic Coastal Plain covers about 60 percent of New Jersey's land area but holds only about one-fourth of the population.

When most people in New Jersey mention southern New Jersey, they are referring to the state's Atlantic coastline, which they call the Shore. This part of the Atlantic Coastal Plain is a long stretch of sandy beaches and barrier islands. The islands are long, narrow sand bars separated by tidal inlets (small waterways) and lagoons. Many of the islands are family-oriented resort communities. Others have nature sanctuaries. In geographic terms, the Jersey Shore is the Outer Coastal Plain. The Inner Coastal Plain is much larger and slightly elevated, though it rarely gets more than 100 feet (30 m) above sea level.

Near the fall line, the Inner Coastal Plain has suburbs and small towns, many dating back to the early 1700s. Campuses for two of the state's best-known universities—Princeton and Rutgers—are located there. The soil is excellent for farming. The northern area of the Coastal Plain has many farms that specialize in tomatoes and other vegetables, including an increasing variety of unusual vegetables from Asia. Some sections are dotted with the white fences and oval tracks of local horse farms.

Horse farms, with their typical white fences, are a common sight in parts of the state's large Coastal Plain region.

The largest area of southern New Jersey's Coastal Plain is a 2,000-square-mile (5,200-sq-km) area called the Pine Barrens, or Pinelands. The soil is not useful for ordinary farming. But the wetland regions are ideal for cranberry bogs, and some drier areas have been turned into blueberry farms. Most of the area is under government protection as the Pinelands National Reserve. The area is home to dozens of rare plant and animal species, including plant varieties that are normally found farther south. Plants that thrive there include pitcher plants and several kinds of bladderworts. These plants are known as "meat eaters" because they trap and digest insects. The Pine Barrens also contain rare species of frogs, turtles, and snakes.

Lined with pine trees, beautiful Pakim Pond lies inside a state forest in the Pinelands National Reserve.

PINELANDS FROG

The beautiful Pine Barrens tree frog likes the white cedar swamps and peat moss of the Pine Barrens. This frog is regarded as a symbol of the Pinelands. It was once considered endangered, but it has done well in recent years. In 2007, the state government upgraded its status from endangered (at risk of dying out) to threatened (at risk of becoming endangered in the near future).

Cape May lies at the southern tip of New Jersey. From Cape May, the Jersey Shore extends northward along some 130 miles (200 km) of beaches and coastal islands. Fifty resort cities and towns, including Atlantic City, draw vacationers in the summer. Sandy Hook, in the north, is a 6.5-mile-long (10.5-km-long) peninsula that stretches into the Atlantic Ocean. Black cherry trees and ancient holly trees provide food for migrating birds. This sandy area is said to be the best place in the nation to observe migrating hawks.

CAPE MAY

One of the nation's oldest summer resorts, Cape May was a vacation spot even before the American Revolution. In the 1800s, it became easily reachable from Philadelphia by steamboat or train. Cape May was once called "the Playground of Presidents." Five U.S. presidents visited there in the nineteenth century. In the 1890s, President Benjamin Harrison made a Cape May hotel his summer White House.

Dozens of people enjoy a winter's day on the frozen surface of Lake Carnegie in Princeton.

Climate

New Jersey measures only 167 miles (269 km) north to south and 56 miles (90 km) wide. But despite the state's small size, its climate varies from one region to another. The coldest areas are in the northwest corner. The average January temperature there is about 28 degrees Fahrenheit (–2 degrees Celsius), and summers are cool because of the higher altitude. In the southwest, the winter temperature is about 34 °F (1 °C). Summers are quite warm, averaging 76 °F (24 °C) in July. The ocean keeps coastal temperatures warmer during winter and cooler in the summer. However, the long, low coastline is sometimes hit by hurricanes and strong winter storms called nor'easters, which sweep in off the Atlantic.

Northern New Jersey gets 40 to 50 inches (101 to 127 centimeters) of snow each year. The southernmost parts of the state get only 10 to 15 inches (25 to 38 cm). The snow can create dangerous driving conditions. But skiing and snowboarding are favorite winter pastimes for many New Jerseyans, and the icy lakes and ponds are ideal for ice-skating and hockey.

Wild New Jersey

The varied landscapes and climate make New Jersey an ideal place for a wide range of plant and animal life. The state boasts nearly fifty state parks and forests. There are also more than one hundred special so-called wildlife management areas. These protected areas offer people a chance to view wildlife sanctuaries from roads, trails, and boardwalks, sometimes within the shadow of high-rise apartments and office buildings.

Beech, cedar, maple, poplar, birch, and oak trees are found across the state. In the fall, leaves change color, turning the landscape into a lovely blend of orange, red, and yellow. In the spring, summer, and fall, flowers bloom across all parts of the state. Flowering plants such as buttercups, azaleas, bloodroot, mountain laurels, and lilies are native to the state. New Jersey's trees, shrubs, and flowers provide both food and homes for wildlife.

Mountain laurels are one of many types of flowering plants native to New Jersey.

Much of New Jersey's wildlife lives in the woodlands found across the state. Most of the animals common to the northeastern United States are found there. These include white-tailed deer, raccoons, opossums, red foxes, coyotes, squirrels, skunks, and rabbits. Porcupines, beavers, and bats also make New Jersey their home. Smaller numbers of black bears and bobcats continue to prowl the heavily wooded hillsides. Sometimes these woodland animals get too close to places where people live. Deer like to eat plants in people's gardens, and raccoons and other animals are interested in people's garbage.

New Jersey is known for its number and variety of birds. The state is on the Atlantic Flyway. This is the route that migrating birds take to their nesting grounds in Central and South America. In addition, the state's mild climate and many sanctuaries and wilderness areas create ideal conditions for nesting. Cape May

White-tailed deer can often be spotted in the state's woods and meadows. Sometimes they even invade backyards.

may be the most famous location in the country for bird-watchers. More than 100,000 bird-watchers visit the area every year, and hundreds of species of birds have been seen there.

The many lakes, ponds, streams, and rivers also provide homes to New Jersey wildlife. Fish such as bass, trout, and pike swim through the waters. Lobsters, crabs, oysters, and clams live in the state's coastal waters. Sometimes whales can be seen moving through the ocean. Ducks, geese, egrets, herons, and pelicans are among the many birds that can be seen wading and swimming in or flying above the state's waterways.

New Jersey is a mixture of rolling hills, sandy beaches, numerous waterways, and dramatic landscapes. The variety of land and water—and diverse plant and animal life—helps make the Garden State a pleasant place that its people are proud to call home.

Bird-watchers can catch sight of many different species at the Cape May Bird Observatory.

A NURSING HOME FOR WILD ANIMALS

The Popcorn Park Zoo, in Forked River, is an unusual place. It was founded in 1977 to keep wild animals that are injured or too old to take care of themselves. The zoo also began taking in domesticated animals, such as circus animals that were abused and Easter rabbits and chicks that were abandoned. People can visit the zoo and see the animals.

Plants & Animals

Opossum

New Jersey's forests provide habitats for the opossum, one of the country's oddest mammals. The opossum's strong tail enables the animal to hang upside down. When trapped on the ground, the opossum may fake being dead until the danger is over. That is where the term "playing possum" comes from.

Orchid

The wetlands of New Jersey's Pine Barrens are home to about twenty species of orchids. Many of these varieties are normally found much farther south.

Prickly Pear

Along the Delaware Water Gap, the hillsides form natural rock gardens. For a few weeks each year, these gardens erupt in bright yellow blossoms. The flowers are from the prickly pear—a cactus that people often associate with the deserts of the Southwest. When the blossoms fade, the cacti produce the purple-pink "pear."

Piping Plover

The small white and brownish piping plover is a common sight at the water's edge along New Jersey beaches. Plovers nest on the ground, so their eggs and offspring are in danger from humans and animals. Even ants can be a threat. These birds began declining in numbers in the late 1940s, as beaches became more developed. Conservation efforts have helped reverse the decline, but plovers are still considered threatened in New Jersey.

Warbler

Southern New Jersey is famous for bird-watching. The many varieties of nesting warblers are especially exciting for bird-watchers. These include yellow-throated, pine, prairie, blue-winged, worm-eating, black-and-white, and Cape May warblers. On a good day, birders can see nearly twenty-five different bird species.

Red Fox

The red fox lost much of its habitat as cities and suburbs spread across the state. But these intelligent little animals are still a common sight in the hills of northwestern New Jersey, in the Highlands region, and in the Pine Barrens. They hunt birds and other prey, mostly by night, and may sometimes threaten livestock. The fox's bushy tail helps cover its tracks in the snow.

From the Beginning

Little is known about the first people who lived in present-day New Jersey. The earliest groups probably arrived in the region about ten thousand years ago. By the year 1600, New Jersey was home to the Lenape people. They hunted, fished, and gathered wild plant foods. They also planted crops, such as beans, squash, corn, and tobacco. They lived in small communities, sometimes built along riverbanks. Their homes, called wigwams, were made out of saplings, bark, and other plant material. The wigwams were small and usually round, though they could be long or oblong. The Lenape used materials such as animal hides, seashells, plants, and clay to make their own clothes, baskets, and pottery. Some Lenape also made swift canoes out of bark and other tree parts.

Quick Facts

AMERICAN INDIAN INFLUENCE

Today, the original Lenape people would hardly recognize the homeland they once called Scheyichbi. Yet many place names in modern New Jersey come from their language. For example, the town of Absecon gets its name from a Lenape word meaning "place of swans." Hohokus is named after the Lenape word for red oak tree. The name *Metuchen* comes from the Lenape word for dry firewood, and *Wanaque* means "land of sassafras," a root that the Lenape used as medicine.

Modern-day Americans reenact the 1778 Battle of Monmouth, one of many battles fought on New Jersey soil during the American Revolution.

Long ago, the Lenape lived in dwellings like this one.

The Lenape were a branch of the Algonquian family of tribes. The Algonquian were among the first American Indians to meet the European explorers who landed on the Atlantic Coast during the 1500s and 1600s. European settlers referred to the Lenape as the Delaware Indians. As European settlement increased, the Delaware were forced off their land. They were pushed to the south and to the west as more white settlers arrived.

Europeans Arrive

The first European explorer to land on the shore of present-day New Jersey was Giovanni da Verrazzano, an Italian sea captain who sailed for France in 1524. Verrazzano, however, did not claim the land for France. Nearly a century passed before Europeans settled in this part of North America.

In 1609, Henry Hudson sailed along the New Jersey coast before entering the river that now bears his name. Hudson was an English explorer who sailed under the flag of the Netherlands. He claimed the area for the Dutch. By 1630, about two hundred Dutch fur trappers and traders had settled along the Atlantic Coast. They soon had rivals in the area—Swedish colonists, who settled in present-day Wilmington, Delaware, in 1638.

The Dutch forced the Swedish colonists to surrender in 1655 and ruled the area as part of their colony of New Netherland. The colony included the town called New Amsterdam at the southern end of Manhattan Island in what is now New York City. It also included other settlements in what is now New York State. By 1660, it also included the settlement that later became Jersey City.

Soon a more powerful rival—England—claimed modern-day New Jersey and the surrounding area as its own. King Charles II of England granted the area to his brother, the Duke of York. In 1664, an English fleet sailed into the harbor of New Amsterdam and demanded the surrender of all of New Netherland. The Dutch governor, Peter Stuyvesant, wanted to defend the colony, but the settlers would not support him. Stuyvesant

In Their Own Words

This is a very good land to fall with, and a pleasant sight to see.

—From the journal of Robert Juet, a member of Henry Hudson's crew, referring to the Jersey Shore

This picture shows English explorer Henry Hudson meeting with Indians along the river that now bears his name.

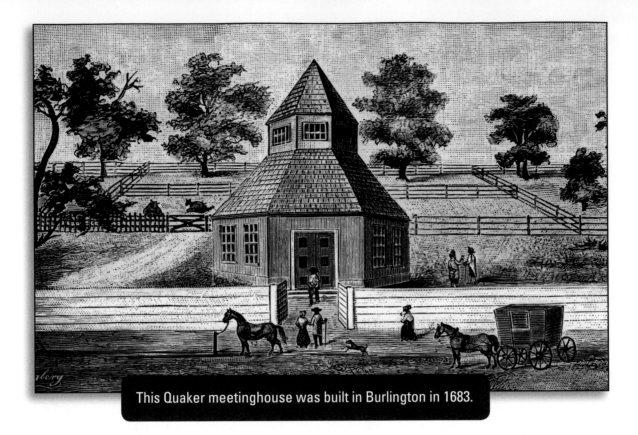

This Quaker meetinghouse was built in Burlington in 1683.

surrendered without a fight. The English renamed the captured Dutch colony New York.

The Duke of York gave the area between the Hudson and Delaware rivers to two friends. One of them, Sir George Carteret, had been governor of the island of Jersey in the English Channel. The new colony was named New Jersey in his honor. Carteret and his friend Lord John Berkeley attracted hundreds of colonists by offering land at very low cost. They also allowed religious freedom and gave people a voice in the government. However, the government was sometimes hostile to certain religious groups, such as Quakers. From 1674 to 1702, New Jersey was divided into East and West Jersey, with separate capitals. In 1702, England reunited the colony. But the two capitals remained until 1775, one at Perth Amboy, the other at Burlington.

The Colonial Years

Throughout the 1700s, New Jersey prospered as a farming colony. Efforts to establish a whaling port in the south were unsuccessful, and business developed slowly. Some colonists thought that New Jersey was doomed to be dominated by the two large cities nearby—Philadelphia to the west and New York to the east. One New Jersey merchant said, "Our wealth ends up in those cities. We are becoming like a keg tapped at both ends."

The people of New Jersey, however, soon found that their location between the two big cities could be a source of strength. As colonial America grew and became prosperous, New Jersey was in a crucial position for moving goods and people between New York and Philadelphia. In the early 1700s, colonial America's first stagecoach service was established across New Jersey to connect the two cities. That was just the beginning. From then on, New Jersey's role as a go-between for Philadelphia and New York steadily expanded.

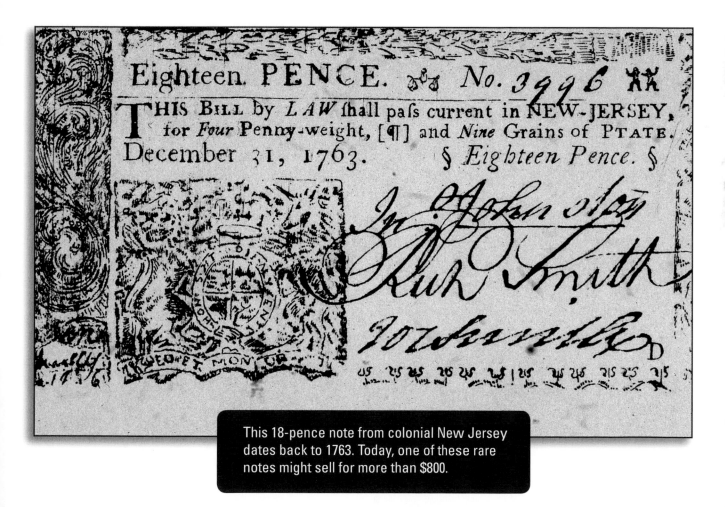

This 18-pence note from colonial New Jersey dates back to 1763. Today, one of these rare notes might sell for more than $800.

MAKING A SOAP CARVING

Many colonial parents gave their children handmade toys. These included dolls, puzzles, and carved toys and figurines. The carvings were usually made of wood that had been carefully whittled. You can make your own carving using a bar of soap.

WHAT YOU NEED

A few pages of newspaper

Paper

Pen

1 large rectangular bar of soap

Clay-carving tools or a plastic knife

Spread some newspaper on your workspace.

Before you start carving, use a separate piece of paper to draw a sketch of the object you would like to create. Once you have decided what your carving will look like, use the pen to lightly draw an outline on the soap.

Have an adult supervise as you use the knife or the clay-carving tools. Be careful: these objects may be sharp.

Begin carving. Take only a little soap off at a time and work slowly. Be sure to carve away from your body. If certain parts of the soap are too hard to carve, ask an adult to help. Be sure not to touch your eyes or your face while handling the soap. After you have finished carving the basic outline of your object, carefully add small details with the points of your tools.

Display your soap carving as a work of art, or use it every time you wash your hands!

The American Revolution

From 1754 to 1763, Great Britain (which had been formed by the union of England and Scotland) fought against France for control of eastern North America. The conflict was known as the French and Indian War. Britain defeated France, but the cost of the war put the British government deeply in debt. As a result, Great Britain tried to tighten its control over trade with its thirteen American colonies and imposed new taxes on the colonies. Many colonists, known as patriots, believed they were too heavily taxed and were not given a fair say in how they were governed.

In 1774, patriots in Greenwich in southwestern New Jersey borrowed an idea from the Boston Tea Party. They protested the British tax on tea by burning a shipload of British tea. The following year, problems between the colonies and Great Britain turned into war. Early fighting broke out in Lexington and Concord in Massachusetts. On July 4, 1776, representatives of the colonies approved the Declaration of Independence. The famous document stated that the colonies now considered themselves free of British rule. The Declaration of Independence was an important step toward making the Thirteen Colonies into one united, independent nation.

The fight against Britain for independence, the American Revolution, lasted from 1775 to 1783. During the war, thousands of New Jerseyans joined the colonies' Continental Army, led by General George Washington. But other New Jerseyans, who called themselves loyalists, wanted to stay under British rule. Some loyalists left their homes in New Jersey to move to areas protected by the British. The governor of New Jersey, William Franklin, was among the loyalists who left. He was the son of Benjamin Franklin, one of the leading patriots and Founding Fathers of the new nation.

New Jersey's location made it a natural battleground. Both sides wanted control of the Hudson and Delaware rivers. Nearly a hundred armed clashes took place in New Jersey, including three major battles: Trenton, Princeton, and Monmouth.

The Battle of Trenton is often regarded as the conflict that saved the patriot cause in its darkest hour. In the autumn of 1776, Washington's Continental Army

This picture shows George Washington and his troops crossing the Delaware River into New Jersey on December 25, 1776. The surprise attack that followed was a big victory for his army in the American Revolution.

had been badly beaten by a powerful British force. After losing New York City and Long Island to the British, Washington and his battered troops retreated. They moved west through New Jersey, crossing the Delaware River into Pennsylvania. By late December, the patriot cause seemed hopeless. Washington's once-proud army of twenty-five thousand now numbered fewer than four thousand. Many did not have winter coats or shoes.

On December 25—Christmas night—Washington led his men back across the ice-clogged Delaware River. At dawn they surprised a regiment of German troops—who had been hired by the British—and won a stunning victory in the Battle of Trenton. A few days later, Washington struck again, defeating the British at the Battle of Princeton. Those two victories gave patriot troops much-needed confidence to keep fighting.

In June 1778, Washington's army fought the British at the Battle of Monmouth. Neither side could claim victory in the battle, but the British were forced to withdraw. The battle showed that the Continental Army could hold its own against the mighty British. Monmouth marked the last time during the American Revolution that two major armies met in battle in New Jersey. However, the two sides fought many smaller battles over the next few years. Life remained difficult for Washington's army. The winter of 1779–1780 is said to have been the coldest of the century. At their camp in Morristown, New Jersey, Washington's men suffered severely from hunger and cold. About a hundred died from the extreme weather.

The war officially ended with the signing of the Treaty of Paris in September 1783. Great Britain recognized the independence of the newly formed United States. The last British troops left American soil a few months later.

This mansion in Morristown served as George Washington's headquarters in the winter of 1779–1780. Today, it is open to the public as part of Morristown National Historical Park.

MOLLY PITCHER

One of the most famous legends of the American Revolution grew out of the Battle of Monmouth. It is said that a heroic wife carried pitchers of water to her husband's unit. When her husband collapsed, the woman helped work one of the cannons for the rest of the battle. She was later called Molly Pitcher. In fact her true identity is not completely certain, and some historians doubt that she even existed.

A New Nation

In the summer of 1787, delegates from twelve of the thirteen former colonies— now states—met at the Constitutional Convention in Philadelphia. (Only Rhode Island did not send any representatives.) The delegates hoped to create a constitution that provided for a strong national government while also protecting the rights of the individual states.

At the convention, New Jersey's William Paterson proposed a single-chamber legislature, or lawmaking body. In Paterson's plan, each state—even a small state such as New Jersey—would have the same number of representatives. His plan was not accepted, but it did contribute to the Great Compromise. This plan created a U.S. Congress with two houses. States with larger populations would have more members in the House of Representatives. But in the Senate, each state would have two senators, regardless of its population. On December 18, 1787, New Jersey ratified, or approved, the U.S. Constitution. By doing so, it became the third state to officially join the United States. In 1790, Trenton was chosen as the new state capital.

New Business and Technology

New Jersey grew and expanded with the other states of the new nation. Agriculture continued to flourish, and transportation and industry became more important. Alexander Hamilton, who served as the first U.S. secretary of the Treasury, planned a model industrial city. The city of Paterson was built at the Great Falls of the Passaic River. The water from the falls was used to create power for nearby factories. These factories used newly developed machines that produced goods quickly and at a low cost. Some of these goods included textiles, tools, and weapons.

In 1804, John Stevens from Hoboken developed a twin-propeller steamboat. In 1811, he launched the nation's first steamboat ferry service, between Hoboken and New York City. In 1825, Stevens created a "steam waggon," which ran on an iron track around his estate. This experiment helped prove that steam railroads were possible. His son Robert Stevens started the country's first steam railroad line in 1831. The Camden and Amboy Railroad used a British locomotive called *John Bull*. The railroad line strengthened the economic ties between New York and Philadelphia. The famous Stevens Institute of Technology, in Hoboken, is named after the family that contributed so much to the development of the state.

The Civil War

During the 1800s, the issue of slavery divided the United States. The plantations in Southern states depended on slaves to work the fields. Northern states, including New Jersey, relied on smaller farms and on industries in which slave labor did not provide a big advantage. Many Northerners also believed that slavery was morally wrong. In 1804, New Jersey voted for gradual emancipation of slaves in the state. Lawmakers decided that all males born into slavery would become free at age twenty-five, and females would become free at age twenty-one. Tensions between the North and South continued to grow and led to the Civil

War (1861–1865). Eleven Southern states seceded from, or left, the Union (that is, the United States) and formed the Confederate States of America.

During the Civil War, more than 80,000 young men from New Jersey wore the dark blue uniforms of the Union army. Factories in the state provided supplies for the Union troops. Some people in New Jersey sided with the Confederacy, but the state as a whole remained loyal to the Union. After years of bloody battles, the Union won the war in 1865. In December of that year, the Thirteenth Amendment to the U.S. Constitution officially ended slavery throughout the United States.

Postwar Economy

The economy of New Jersey continued to grow. Silk processing and other industries developed in Paterson. Oil production became important in Bayonne, and Camden became a center for shipbuilding.

The period from the 1860s to the 1890s was known as the Age of the Robber Barons. The robber barons were powerful business leaders such as John D. Rockefeller, who made a fortune in the oil industry, and Andrew Carnegie, who did the same in the steel industry. They accumulated great wealth by creating monopolies in their fields. A monopoly is a company that controls so much of an industry that it has no competition and can charge high prices for its goods or services.

Female workers, like those shown here weaving silk, helped make New Jersey a center of the textile industry for many years.

New Jersey governor Woodrow Wilson casts his ballot on Election Day in 1912. Wilson won the presidential election.

New Jersey politicians saw the rise of these powerful companies as a great opportunity. The state legislature passed laws that encouraged big corporations to set up offices in New Jersey. Monopolies were illegal in other states, but New Jersey allowed them. By the late 1800s, roughly half the nation's largest corporations had established headquarters in New Jersey.

The 1900s and Beyond

The American people became upset with the spread of monopolies. In the early 1900s, President Theodore Roosevelt and other reformers worked to break up these powerful companies. In New Jersey, the reform leader was Woodrow Wilson. He served first as president of Princeton University and then as governor of New Jersey. Wilson was elected president of the United States in 1912 and was reelected in 1916. In 1917, he led the nation into World War I.

New Jersey played an important role during World War I and World War II, which the United States entered in 1941. Hundred of thousands of troops trained and gathered at Camp Dix (later Fort Dix) and other facilities in the state before heading off to war. The state's industries produced wartime products, including chemicals, weapons, ships, and aircraft engines. New Jersey also became a leader in military research and technology.

Quick Facts

AMERICA'S FIRST "HOLLYWOOD"
In the early twentieth century, Fort Lee, New Jersey, was the movie capital of the world. From about 1907 to 1917, most of the biggest movies were made there. Many Wild West scenes were shot near the Palisades. Eventually moviemakers headed to Hollywood, California, where the weather and open spaces made filming much easier.

After World War II, many white people from Newark, Trenton, and other New Jersey cities began to move to surrounding areas, called suburbs. This shift was fueled by a boom in auto sales. To keep up with the growing number of vehicles on the road, New Jersey built two major roadways in the 1950s. Completed in 1951, the New Jersey Turnpike quickly became one of the busiest highways in the country. The Garden State Parkway connected the busy northern suburbs with resort areas along the Atlantic Coast.

As suburbs prospered, many cities in New Jersey began to crumble. Many African Americans either could not afford to move to other areas or were not allowed to move because of discrimination. Some manufacturing plants moved out of the cities as well, taking away jobs and tax revenues. City governments could not maintain important services. Living conditions in cities got worse, and tension between blacks and whites increased. Riots broke out in Newark and other cities in the late 1960s.

American soldiers rejoice as they leave Camp Dix at the end of World War I.

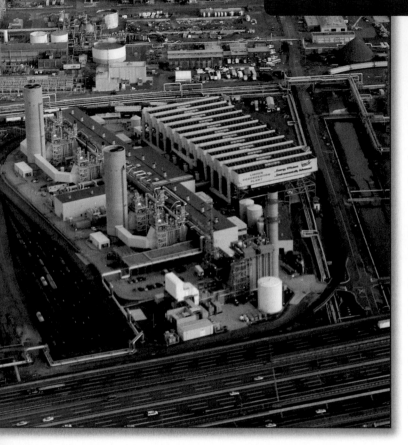

The New Jersey Turnpike passes through a heavily industrial area in the northeastern part of the state.

New Jersey Today

After an economic slump in the mid–1990s, the urban areas of New Jersey began to recover. Along the Hudson River, decaying wharfs and empty warehouses were replaced by modern townhouses, apartment buildings, offices, and shopping malls. Rotting piers and junk heaps gave way to parks, small-boat harbors, and recreation areas. Dozens of New York City companies moved to these renewed areas.

New Jerseyans have fought to reduce the bad effects of industrialization and development and have worked to protect the environment. In 2007, for example, the state passed a law requiring a 20 percent cut in greenhouses gas emissions by the year 2020. Greenhouse gases such as carbon dioxide contribute to global warming—the slow rise in worldwide temperatures.

The severe recession, or economic downturn, that hit the nation in 2008 had a strong impact on New Jersey. Businesses closed and many jobs were lost. Like all states, New Jersey will continue to face challenges. But the recent revival of city areas and the success of preservation efforts offer hope that residents can continue to improve New Jersey's urban areas, while preserving garden areas and open spaces.

Important Dates

★ **1524** Giovanni da Verrazzano explores the New Jersey coast for France.

★ **1609** Henry Hudson lands at modern-day Sandy Hook and claims the area for the Netherlands.

★ **1660** The Dutch establish a permanent settlement near present-day Jersey City.

★ **1664** The English take control of New Jersey.

★ **1674** The New Jersey colony is split into East Jersey and West Jersey.

★ **1702** The two halves are reunited to form a single colony.

★ **1787** New Jersey becomes the third state when it ratifies the U.S. Constitution on December 18.

★ **1846** The first baseball game with rules similar to current ones is played in Hoboken.

★ **1879** Thomas Edison invents the first workable light bulb.

★ **1912** New Jersey governor Woodrow Wilson is elected president of the United States. He is reelected in 1916.

★ **1921** New Jersey and New York create what is now called the Port Authority of New York and New Jersey to develop and operate transportation and port facilities.

★ **1928** The airport now called Newark Liberty International Airport opens. At the time, it was the biggest airport in the world.

★ **1937** The airship *Hindenburg* crashes and burns at Lakehurst, apparently when a spark ignites the airship's hydrogen.

★ **1951** The New Jersey Turnpike opens.

★ **1978** The first gambling casinos open in Atlantic City.

★ **1994** Christine Todd Whitman becomes the first female governor of New Jersey.

★ **2001** Almost 700 New Jerseyans are killed in the September 11 terrorist attacks on the World Trade Center in New York City.

★ **2007** The Prudential Center, a $375-million sports and entertainment arena, opens in Newark.

3

The People

The population of New Jersey exploded during the 1900s. The growth continued into the twenty-first century. The 2000 Census showed that New Jersey's population had grown almost 9 percent in ten years—from 7.7 million people in 1990 to 8.4 million in 2000. In 2007, the population was estimated at close to 8.7 million. New Jersey—already the most crowded state in the nation—was becoming even more crowded. But the population is spread around unevenly. The southern part of the state still has wide-open stretches of farms, forests, and marshland.

New Jersey is one of the most diverse states in the nation. The state has larger percentages of African Americans, Asians, and Hispanics or Latinos than the nation as a whole. People from many different cultures make the Garden State their home.

The First Residents

Before Europeans and other settlers came to the region, American Indians were the only people to live on the land. Most of them were Lenape (later known as the Delaware).

> ## In Their Own Words
>
> *In South Jersey, you still see more birds than people.*
>
> —Steven Lincoln, a state forest guide

New Jersey's diverse population enriches the state.

A young boy performs a hoop dance at the American Indian Arts Festival at the Rankokus Indian Reservation in Burlington County, New Jersey.

As non-native settlements developed and spread, New Jersey's American Indians were pushed off their land. They moved west toward modern-day Ohio. Some traveled as far as Oklahoma.

Today, there are fewer than 20,000 American Indians in the state of New Jersey. They make up far less than 1 percent of the population. Their small population does not keep them from making a difference, however. Like other minority groups, they have struggled against discrimination and worked hard to secure their rightful place in society.

Keeping their history and culture alive is very important to many American Indians. They learn traditional music, dances, ceremonies, and crafts. They also want to share their culture and traditions with others. For example, the Nanticoke Lenni–Lenape of New Jersey host an annual powwow that is open to everyone. Another American Indian group, the Powhatan Renape Nation, maintains the Rankokus Indian Reservation in Burlington County. Visitors can tour a museum of American Indian heritage and see historical artifacts and a reconstructed Indian village. The Powhatan Renape also sponsor festivals that feature art shows, traditional dance competitions, and other events.

Coming to New Jersey

Over the past few centuries, New Jersey's population has undergone changes similar to those in other parts of the Northeast. More than three-quarters of the colonists in New Jersey in the 1700s could trace their origins to Great Britain and Ireland. The same was true of the people in New York and the New England colonies. Many Dutch and Swedish settlers and their descendants also made New Jersey their home.

After 1800, shiploads of immigrants from Europe arrived at New Jersey ports and other ports throughout the Northeast. In the 1840s, the numbers of immigrants increased dramatically, especially from Ireland and Germany. In Ireland, a blight, or disease, struck the potato crop. Potatoes were the major source of food and income for many people. The countryside was devastated, and more than a million people lost their lives. Others escaped the famine on ships bound for the United States. During the same period, large numbers of German immigrants fled from the political problems in their homeland to start new lives in the United States.

Many of the new immigrants headed for New Jersey cities, hoping to find factory jobs. They often met angry opposition from native-born Americans. Some people disliked the newcomers' unfamiliar customs and were afraid that immigrants would take jobs away from them. Gradually, the newcomers overcame the prejudice and fear. Many young Irish women found jobs as household servants. Some German families opened restaurants, butcher shops, and "beer gardens." Other immigrants worked in factories, hospitals, and stores. Many became firefighters or police officers or joined the clergy. Some pursued higher education. Despite limited opportunities, they became lawyers, doctors, writers, and teachers. Some eventually became active in politics.

ELLIS ISLAND

Many of the immigrants who came to New Jersey in the late nineteenth and early twentieth century entered the United States through the Great Hall at Ellis Island (right) in New York Harbor. Just east of Jersey City, Ellis Island had the U.S. government's largest center for receiving immigrants. Many of the immigrants who left Ellis Island took a ferry to Jersey City. Some stayed, and many others took trains from the city's train station to what would be their new homes elsewhere in New Jersey or throughout the United States. Ellis Island itself is located partly in New Jersey and partly in New York State.

The 1880s started a new period of immigration. More people were coming to the United States than ever before. Many arrived from other parts of Europe, such as Russia and what is now Poland. Large numbers of immigrants from Italy settled in New Jersey. The state's population continued to increase through the 1900s and beyond, as more people made the Garden State their home.

Since the early 1970s, New Jersey's population has become even more diverse. Changes in the nation's immigration laws led to an increase in new arrivals from regions other than Europe. In recent decades, people from Spanish-speaking countries in Latin America and people from Asian countries have come to New Jersey in larger numbers than before.

According to Census Bureau estimates, in 2007 approximately 70 percent of New Jersey's population was white. This group includes descendants of Europeans who settled in New Jersey, as well as people with European backgrounds who moved to New Jersey from other states. People of Italian, Irish, German, Polish, and English heritage are among the largest groups of New Jerseyans with European backgrounds.

Hispanics are the largest minority group in New Jersey. They make up about one-sixth of the state's population, and their numbers are growing. More than half the Hispanics in the state are under the age of thirty. Hudson and Passaic counties in northern New Jersey

are the counties with the largest Hispanic populations. Hispanics make up 41 percent of the population of Hudson County and 35 percent of Passaic County's population.

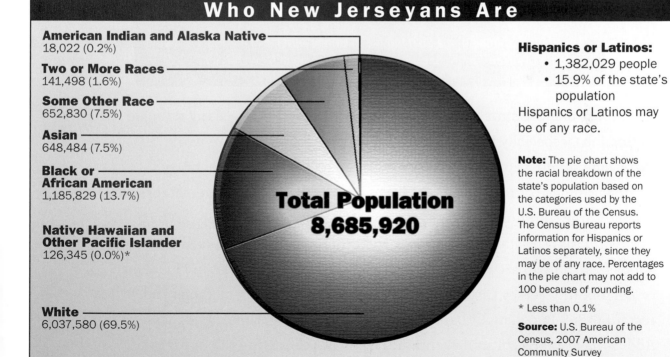

Who New Jerseyans Are

American Indian and Alaska Native
18,022 (0.2%)

Two or More Races
141,498 (1.6%)

Some Other Race
652,830 (7.5%)

Asian
648,484 (7.5%)

Black or African American
1,185,829 (13.7%)

Native Hawaiian and Other Pacific Islander
126,345 (0.0%)*

White
6,037,580 (69.5%)

Total Population 8,685,920

Hispanics or Latinos:
- 1,382,029 people
- 15.9% of the state's population

Hispanics or Latinos may be of any race.

Note: The pie chart shows the racial breakdown of the state's population based on the categories used by the U.S. Bureau of the Census. The Census Bureau reports information for Hispanics or Latinos separately, since they may be of any race. Percentages in the pie chart may not add to 100 because of rounding.

* Less than 0.1%

Source: U.S. Bureau of the Census, 2007 American Community Survey

These boys, studying at a Sikh temple in Bridgewater, are among a growing number of Asian Americans who make their home in New Jersey.

Almost half the state's Hispanic people are foreign-born. Many struggle to find jobs, especially in hard times, or earn low wages for hard work. But increasing numbers of Hispanics are business owners and professionals.

The influence of many different immigrant cultures can be seen across New Jersey. Large communities of people from the same ethnic group can be found in cities across the state. Restaurants and other businesses that sell food and goods from abroad are very popular. A walk down a main street in Hoboken or neighboring Jersey City can reveal a worldwide sampling of shops and restaurants—Brazilian, Cuban, South African, Chinese, Greek, and Sicilian. Additionally, many cultural events and festivals celebrating the heritage of different ethnic groups are held throughout the state.

Hispanics are the largest minority group in the state today. This family is shopping for groceries in Passaic.

African Americans in New Jersey

In the 1800s, African Americans made up only a small portion of New Jersey's population. As slavery in the state came to an end, free African Americans worked at different types of jobs. A few owned farms, and a larger number worked as farm laborers. Even after the Civil War ended, life was often hard for them. Jobs were scarce, and prejudice was widespread.

The United States fought in World Wars I and II in the first half of the twentieth century. New Jersey's factories and shipyards had to quickly manufacture the weapons and equipment needed by America's military forces. Thousands of African Americans moved north from Southern

Quick Facts

SLAVERY IN NEW JERSEY
According to Census Bureau data, there were 12,422 slaves in New Jersey in 1800. New Jersey was the last Northern state to abolish slavery, which it did gradually and in stages starting in 1804.

A community leader urges residents to remain calm as riots shake the city of Newark in July 1967.

states to find work. Many African Americans found jobs as laborers. Over the years, others became scholars, doctors, lawyers, teachers, business owners, and entertainers.

For twenty years after the end of World War II in 1945, the United States enjoyed one of its greatest periods of prosperity. Many people moved to growing New Jersey suburbs, leaving the crowded, congested cities behind. But few African-American families could afford such a move. Prejudiced white people and real estate agencies in mostly white suburban areas often would not rent or sell homes to African Americans. Most cities and suburbs were segregated, meaning that black families could find housing only in black neighborhoods.

The frustrations of African Americans increased during the civil rights movement of the 1950s and 1960s. Martin Luther King Jr. led protest marches through the South. He and other civil rights leaders helped force Southern cities and states to remove laws that discriminated against African Americans. Racial tensions existed in Northern states, too. In the late 1960s, race

African Americans make up a large segment of New Jersey's population.

riots broke out in Northern cities. One of the worst riots occurred in Newark in July 1967. Twenty-six people were killed and more than one thousand were wounded. Rioters caused more than $10 million in property damage.

Like other Northern states, New Jersey launched programs to try to modernize cities and create more opportunities for African Americans. More housing for low-income people was built. New state colleges had lower tuition fees, making them more affordable to New Jerseyans from all walks of life. A commuter railroad improved transportation, and job-training programs were established to help workers develop new skills.

Today, African Americans make up about one-seventh of the state's population. Like other minority groups, they contribute a great deal to New Jersey. African Americans are very active in the politics, education, and businesses of the state.

In Their Own Words

If you think about it, besides some rural areas, inner cities are the last great challenge to this country, to be what [the country] says it is.

—Newark mayor Cory Booker

Famous New Jerseyans

Thomas Edison: Inventor

Thomas Edison was born in 1847 in Ohio and was raised mostly in Michigan. But he spent most of his life in New Jersey. In Menlo Park and then in West Orange, Edison worked in what he called his invention factory. With a small team of helpers, he turned out more than a thousand inventions, including the phonograph, the first long-lasting electric light bulb, and all the basic equipment of the motion-picture industry. The town of Edison, New Jersey, is named in his honor.

Dorothea Lange: Photographer

Born in Hoboken in 1895, Dorothea Lange was a world-famous photographer who used her skills to help people. During the Great Depression of the 1930s, she traveled across the country and took pictures of both the beauty and the despair that she saw. Her vivid photographs called attention to the harsh lives of many people in those years. She died in 1965.

Edwin "Buzz" Aldrin: Astronaut

Born in Montclair in 1930, Buzz Aldrin became a decorated fighter pilot during the Korean War (1950–1953). He later became an astronaut. His spacewalk in 1966 was the longest and most successful at that time. On July 20, 1969, Aldrin became only the second person to set foot on the moon.

Bruce Springsteen: Musician

Bruce Springsteen was born in 1949 in Freehold, a mill town in Monmouth County. He became one of the biggest rock musicians of the 1970s and 1980s. His music often reflects the hardships and hopes of everyday working people. "The Boss" is still very popular around the world and has influenced countless other musicians.

Cory Booker: Politician

Born in 1969, Cory Booker grew up in Harrington Park, New Jersey. He was a top athlete and student. He played football at Stanford University, and he graduated from Yale Law School in 1997. Booker became active in helping less-fortunate, low-income people in Newark's inner city. He was elected to the city council in 1998. In 2006, he was elected mayor of the troubled city. He has worked hard to tackle problems such as poverty and crime.

The Jonas Brothers: Musicians

Kevin (born in 1987), Joseph (1989), and Nick (1992) Jonas all grew up in Wyckoff. Nick started singing in Broadway shows when he was only six. The brothers made their first album in 2006 and starred in the Disney Channel movie *Camp Rock* two years later. In 2009, they went on their first world tour and also entertained President Barack Obama's two daughters, Malia and Sasha, at the White House.

Living in New Jersey

Why do people live in New Jersey? That is a question with many answers. Many move to the state because of the job opportunities it offers. Large corporations have been based in New Jersey for a long time. Recently, more corporate offices and research companies have moved out of New York City to New Jersey to take advantage of greater space, lower rents, and lower taxes. These businesses create jobs in factories, offices, and stores.

New Jersey's location is attractive to commuters. Many New Jerseyans live in suburbs outside cities where they work. People call these suburbs "bedroom communities"—places where city workers sleep. Several bridges and tunnels cross the Hudson River to New York City, and bridges span the Delaware River to Philadelphia. Commuters can travel by train, bus, or car, and some can conveniently cross the Hudson River by ferry. Highways may be crowded and trips may be long, but for many commuters, living in New Jersey is worth the trouble.

Other residents enjoy the quiet, country life offered by farmland in the south. The shoreline is popular with people who enjoy the ocean and beaches.

Many people are drawn to New Jersey by its schools. Some New Jersey schools are among the highest-rated in the nation. New Jersey is also home to fine universities and colleges that attract students from across the country and around the world.

Quick Facts

TUNNEL VISION

Each year, almost 50 million vehicles travel between New York and New Jersey through the Holland and Lincoln tunnels. The Holland Tunnel opened in 1927. The Lincoln Tunnel followed ten years later. Before the Holland Tunnel was built, people relied only on ferries to get across the Hudson River.

Like all states, New Jersey is not perfect. Poverty and crime are problems in some areas. When economic times are hard, more and more people lose their jobs, and state and local governments have trouble balancing their budgets while providing the services that people need. But to most of the state's ever-changing population, living in New Jersey has many benefits.

Many New Jerseyans commute to New York City across the George Washington Bridge, which was built over the Hudson River in 1931. More than 100 million vehicles travel the bridge each year.

Calendar of Events

★ Super Science Weekend

Held early in the year at the State Museum in Trenton, the Super Science Weekend features exhibits and hands-on activities for kids of all ages.

★ Annual Shad Festival

Every spring, the shad, a type of fish, start their run up the Delaware River to spawn. The shad run is an exciting time for people who like to fish or just enjoy the once-a-year fish feast.

★ Wildwood International Kite Festival

Kite builders and competitors from as far away as Japan come to Wildwood on Memorial Day weekend to show off many kinds of colorful kites.

★ Annual Battle of Monmouth

In late June, hundreds of people in period costume re-create the American Revolution battle at Monmouth. The actors use muskets and other authentic equipment to help show how General Washington saved the day for the Americans.

★ New Jersey Festival of Ballooning

Each July, dozens of colorful hot air balloons brighten the skies above Readington in the north-central part of the state. Balloon enthusiasts come from all parts of the country.

★ New Jersey State Fair/Sussex County Farm and Horse Show

The state fair and horse show is a big event in the middle of the summer. It is held at the Sussex County Fairgrounds in Augusta. Highlights include everything from fruit and vegetable competitions and racing pigs to wood-chopping contests and carnival rides.

★ Hummingbird Extravaganza

The Hummingbird Extravaganza is held in Swainton in August. The popular event provides demonstrations of how to attract these tiny birds to backyard gardens.

★ Victorian Week in Cape May

Cape May is noted for its many old-fashioned houses and inns from the time of Britain's Queen Victoria (1837–1901). Visitors can tour these remarkable buildings and enjoy other events during this ten-day celebration in October.

★ Cranberry Festival

The Cranberry Festival is held in Chatsworth in October. It celebrates cranberries—an important crop in the state—and shows off many ways to use them.

★ Reenactment of Washington's Crossing of the Delaware

This event re-creates Washington's famous crossing on Christmas night 1776, which was followed by the victory of the Continental Army at the Battle of Trenton. It is meant to be an annual event, but sometimes the current is too strong for the actors to safely cross the river.

4

How the Government Works

Every state has different layers of government. From the smallest village to the largest city, nearly every community has a government. There are more than five hundred of these communities—or municipalities—in New Jersey. These include cities, towns, townships, boroughs, and villages. Most cities are governed by a mayor and a city council. There are many other local bodies with important powers, such as school boards, planning boards, zoning boards, and water commissions.

Cities, towns, and townships are grouped together to form counties. New Jersey has twenty-one counties. They are governed by groups called boards of chosen freeholders. This term dates back to colonial times, when only men who owned property, called freeholders, could vote or hold office. The counties handle a wide variety of responsibilities, involving schools, roads, hospitals, and other key areas.

The next level is state government. The governor, the governor's staff, the legislature, and the judicial system work together to create and uphold laws and run the government. New Jersey has a large degree of "home rule," That means that under the state's constitution and laws, local governments have more power than they do in many other states.

Through 2010, New Jersey also had fifteen representatives in the U.S. Congress in Washington, D.C. Voters in New Jersey elected thirteen members

The governor, state legislature, and several government agencies
have offices in the New Jersey State House in Trenton.

Branches of Government

EXECUTIVE ★ ★ ★ ★ ★ ★ ★ ★

The governor and lieutenant governor are elected to four-year terms. Other officials such as the attorney general, secretary of state, and treasurer, are appointed by the governor.

LEGISLATIVE ★ ★ ★ ★ ★ ★ ★ ★

The legislature is made up of two houses: the senate and the general assembly. The senate has forty members, and the general assembly has eighty. Members of the assembly are elected every two years. Senators serve four-year terms, except the first term of a new decade, which is only two years.

JUDICIAL ★ ★ ★ ★ ★ ★ ★ ★ ★

The court system has several divisions. Municipal courts hear cases for minor offenses, such as traffic tickets and shoplifting. Municipal judges are appointed by the local government. Each county has a superior court, which hears cases involving criminal, civil, and family law. People who do not agree with the outcome of their case can have it reviewed by an appellate court. New Jersey also has a tax court. The supreme court is the highest court in the state and hears the most important cases. Judges for the superior, tax, and supreme courts are selected by the governor and must be approved by the state senate. Each of these judge's term is seven years.

to the U.S. House of Representatives. Like voters in all other states, they also elect two U.S. senators.

How a Bill Becomes a Law

Ideas for new state laws often come from concerned citizens, but any proposed law, called a bill, must be officially submitted by an assembly member or a senator. A committee studies the bill and may amend, or change, it. Committees have public meetings where people from the community may speak about the bill. If the committee approves it, the bill is then debated in the house in which it was first proposed. Legislators may argue about the bill and amend it further.

A bill passes if it receives a majority of the vote—twenty-one votes if it is in the senate or forty-one if it is in the general assembly. If enough members of one

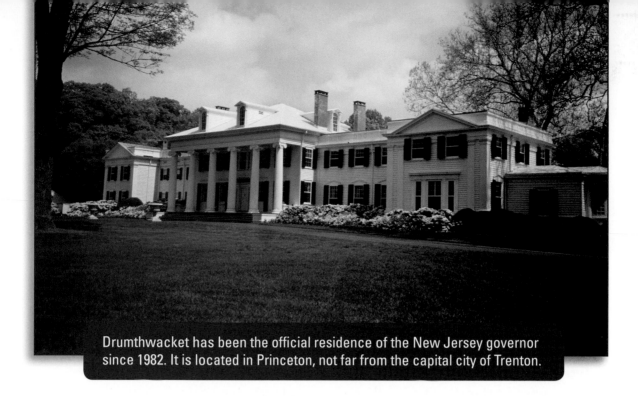

Drumthwacket has been the official residence of the New Jersey governor since 1982. It is located in Princeton, not far from the capital city of Trenton.

house vote for the bill, it is sent to the other house, where it goes through a similar process. If the second house approves the bill, it goes on to the governor. The governor can approve the bill or may decide to veto, or reject, it. If the governor does not take any action on the bill, it can become a law. If the governor vetoes the bill, it can still become law if two-thirds of both the senate and the general assembly vote for it.

Both legislative houses can also propose amendments to the state constitution. If three-fifths of the assembly and the senate approve the amendment, it goes on the ballot in the next general election. The amendment passes if the majority of voters approve it. The current state constitution has been amended more than thirty times.

New Jersey Politics

New Jersey's strong emphasis on home rule has encouraged many citizens to make their views known to local and state officials. Citizens may also run for many types of local office. Many of these positions are unpaid, but they offer the person a role in making decisions that affect the community. However, some people say that New Jersey has too many local bodies that have too much

Contacting Lawmakers

★ ★ ★ ★ ★ ★ ★ ★ ★ ★ ★ ★ ★ ★

To contact New Jersey state legislators, visit this website:

http://www.njleg.state.nj.us/members/legsearch.asp

You may search by town (municipality) to find the people who represent that area in the state legislature.

power. Over the years, New Jersey officials have sometimes abused these powers. Some were convicted of accepting bribes in return for granting contracts or giving favorable treatment to certain businesses.

New Jersey lawmakers have made many decisions of importance to people in the state. Some of them have been controversial. For example, in 1978, the state legislature passed a law to permit gambling in the resort town of Atlantic City. While some people opposed this decision, the move created new income for the government. Much of the money is used to finance

In July 2009, the federal government announced the arrests of more than forty New Jerseyans, including several politicians, on charges of corruption.

Since 1978, when gambling became legal in Atlantic City, the city's casinos have brought in tax revenue that helps fund state government programs.

programs for the elderly, people with disabilities, the homeless, and people with low incomes.

Other measures have been less controversial. For example, in 2010, the state passed a law aimed at reducing the number of pedestrians who are killed in traffic accidents. The law requires drivers to come to a full stop whenever a pedestrian begins to cross a street at a crosswalk. It also increases the penalty for "jaywalking," or crossing a street when and where it is not allowed.

Quick Facts

THE LIEUTENANT GOVERNOR

For a long time, New Jersey was one of the few states that had no lieutenant governor. The lieutenant governor is like the vice president of the state. In 2001 and again in 2004, the governor of New Jersey resigned and was replaced by the person who was president of the senate. Then, in November 2005, New Jersey voters approved an amendment to the constitution that created the position of lieutenant governor. Starting in 2009, the lieutenant governor runs for office on the same ticket with the governor. The lieutenant governor takes over if the governor resigns or dies in office.

5

Making a Living

New Jersey's economy is as diverse as its population. Fields such as agriculture, research, manufacturing, service, and tourism bring money into the state and provide jobs for its residents.

Agriculture

Much of New Jersey is covered with cities and suburbs, and large areas are protected for wetlands or wildlife preserves. Yet close to 20 percent of the land area is still devoted to farmland.

There are about ten thousand farms in the state. Most are fairly small and family-owned. Prosperous dairy farms and orchards cover the hillsides of the northwestern corner of the state. In the northeastern corner of New Jersey, greenhouses and nurseries produce many types of colorful flowers. Many flowers grown there end up in New York City markets. On the level lands just north of the Pine Barrens, truck farms produce a variety of vegetables, especially tomatoes, sweet corn, lettuce, and beans. New Jersey's Pine Barrens are home to the largest cranberry bogs outside New England. New Jersey is also one of the top blueberry-growing states.

Although fishing is not a major New Jersey industry, the long coast is an excellent source of clams. The coastal waters are also good for catching flounder, lobsters, and oysters.

A farmer harvests floating cranberries from a bog in the Pine Barrens. New Jersey has the nation's biggest cranberry bogs outside New England.

RECIPE FOR BLUEBERRY MUFFINS

"Pick your own" berry farms can be found all over the Garden State. The Pinelands, a marshy part of the state, are ideal for growing blueberries. These muffins are one of the many tasty treats you can make with plump, sweet New Jersey blueberries.

WHAT YOU NEED

$1\frac{1}{4}$ cup (140 grams) regular flour

$\frac{3}{4}$ cup (177 milliliters) skim milk

$\frac{3}{4}$ cup (85 g) whole wheat flour

1 egg white

$2\frac{3}{4}$ teaspoons (14 g) baking powder

3 tablespoons (44 ml) honey

$\frac{1}{4}$ teaspoon (1.5 g) baking soda

3 tablespoons (44 ml) oil

$\frac{1}{3}$ cup (75 g) sugar

$1\frac{1}{4}$ teaspoons (6 ml) vanilla extract

1 cup (150 g) fresh blueberries

Ask an adult to help you preheat the oven to 425 °F (218 °C). Grease the cups in a twelve-muffin pan and set aside the pan.

Sift the two kinds of flour, the baking powder, and the baking soda into a bowl. Add the sugar and the blueberries. Gently mix.

In a separate bowl, combine the milk, egg white, honey, oil, and vanilla. Pour the liquid mixture into the flour mixture. Mix them together to form the muffin batter.

Pour the batter evenly into the twelve muffin cups. Have an adult carefully place the pan in the oven. Bake the muffins for 13 to 16 minutes at 425 °F (218 °C).

Let the muffins cool for at least five minutes before removing them from the pan.

Research

New Jersey is known as the state where the famed inventor Thomas Alva Edison had his laboratories. The state is also the home of the Institute for Advanced Study in Princeton, where the scientific genius Albert Einstein did research from the mid–1930s to the mid–1950s. Other well-known research organizations with facilities in New Jersey include Bell Laboratories and Western Electric. Many drug companies, computer companies, and aerospace research firms are also based in the state. The large pharmaceutical and health-care products company Johnson & Johnson has its headquarters in New Brunswick and has research centers and offices elsewhere in the state.

Albert Einstein, perhaps the greatest scientific genius of the twentieth century, did research for twenty years at the Institute for Advanced Study in Princeton.

Manufacturing

New Jersey has a long industrial history. The state has been a leader in industrial development since the mid–1800s. Smoke once hung over the cities as machines churned out an incredible variety of products in large quantities—shoes, machine parts, chemicals, furniture, and dozens of other items. During both world wars, New Jersey turned its industrial might to the production of weapons and ammunition. The state has been losing manufacturing jobs in recent years, but some areas are growing. Manufacturing jobs in the state often require special skills, and they usually pay well.

Today, New Jersey is the national leader in making drugs and other

A technician wearing a sterile suit carefully handles a tray of glass vials in a medical lab. New Jersey is a major center for the manufacture of drugs and medical products.

medical products, its biggest manufacturing industry. The related field of biotechnology has become a key industry, too. Biotechnology is the use of biological materials and processes to make useful products, such as pharmaceuticals.

Another big area is the production of chemicals, including such household products as cleansers, soaps, and shampoos.

Computer and electronic products have grown in importance. New Jersey is also one of the top states in food processing, including freezing and canning foods and producing wholesale baked goods.

At Your Service

Like that of other states, New Jersey's economy has become increasingly geared toward service industries. About three of every five New Jersey workers has a job in this sector. Service industries include transportation, education, health care, banking, and insurance. People who work in retail stores, restaurants, and hotels are also part of the service industry.

Shipping

The Port of New York and New Jersey is the largest port on the East Coast and third-largest in the United States (behind the ports in Houston, Texas, and in southern Louisiana). Major port facilities, operated by the Port Authority of New York and New Jersey, are located in Newark, Elizabeth, and Jersey City, as well as in New York City. In 2008, more than $190 billion worth of cargo entered or left the United States through the Port of New York and New Jersey. The port provides jobs for thousands of New Jersey workers.

Workers & Industries

Industry	Number of People Working in That Industry	Percentage of All Workers Who Are Working in That Industry
Education and health care	911,775	21.4%
Wholesale and retail businesses	640,198	15.1%
Professionals, scientists, and managers	507,206	11.9%
Publishing, media, entertainment, hotels, and restaurants	461,425	10.8%
Banking and finance, insurance, and real estate	398,212	9.4%
Manufacturing	393,453	9.3%
Construction	280,643	6.6%
Transportation and public utilities	257,900	6.1%
Government	195,627	4.6%
Other services	189,631	4.5%
Farming, fishing, forestry	16,976	0.4%
Totals	4,253,046	100%

Notes: Figures above do not include people in the armed forces. "Professionals" includes people such as doctors and lawyers. Percentages may not add to 100 because of rounding.

Source: U.S. Bureau of the Census, 2007 estimates

Tourism

Throughout the state's history, people have visited New Jersey to enjoy all it has to offer. Today, tourist activities bring in close to $40 billion in revenue each year, and tourism provides jobs for one in nine New Jersey workers.

Tourism got a big boost after casino gambling became legal in Atlantic City in 1978. The city's hotels and famous boardwalk had made it a popular vacation spot for a hundred years, but it had been in decline in recent decades. Once gambling was permitted, developers and investors moved in to create glittering resorts that rivaled those in Las Vegas. But there is more to Atlantic City than gambling. Families go to see shows, stroll along the boardwalk, and enjoy the sun and

MONOPOLY

In 1934, during the Great Depression, Charles Darrow, an out-of-work salesman, sold a game he called Monopoly to the Parker Brothers game company. The properties on the board were all named after real streets in Atlantic City. Although many people say Darrow did not invent the game himself, he helped make it one of the most successful board games in history. Today, at the real corner of Boardwalk and Park Place, a brass plaque honors Darrow for his achievement.

Children enjoy a thrilling ride on the Crazy Mouse roller coaster at the Steel Pier on the Atlantic City boardwalk.

THE ULTIMATE THRILL RIDE

People who love theme park thrills flock to Six Flags Great Adventure in Jackson Township. Great Adventure is home to Kingda Ka, the tallest and fastest roller coaster in the world. Its top speed is 128 miles (206 km) per hour, and its tallest hill reaches 456 feet (139 m) high. That is taller than the Statue of Liberty.

sand of the beaches. About 30 million guests now visit the city each year. A big portion of the money spent in Atlantic City goes back to the state.

People visit New Jersey's cities to attend plays, movies, and concerts. The state's museums are widely respected. The state has a battleship museum, an agricultural museum, and many historical museums and historical sites. Of course, the Garden State also has many beautiful public gardens.

The Liberty Science Center in Jersey City features exhibits and hands-on activities, as well as educational programs for students. The center is located in Liberty State Park, on the western shore of Upper New York Bay. Ferries from Liberty State Park take visitors to the Statue of Liberty and to Ellis Island.

The Liberty Science Center in Jersey City attracts visitors of all ages with its many hands-on activities.

Martin Brodeur of the New Jersey Devils tends the net in an October 2009 hockey game at Newark's Prudential Center.

The Jersey Shore continues to draw millions of visitors each summer. From Sandy Hook in the north to Cape May at the state's southern tip, visitors come to splash in the waves and lounge on the beach. Over the years, resorts and businesses that cater to shore visitors have brought in big money for the state.

Sports fans have plenty to cheer about in New Jersey. The New Jersey Devils, the state's pro hockey team, play at the Prudential Center in Newark. The state's pro basketball team, the Nets, moved to the Prudential Center in 2010. The Jets and the Giants football teams may represent New York, but they play their home games at the Meadowlands. A new $1.6-billion stadium at the Meadowlands for the two teams opened in 2010. The Meadowlands are also home to one of three major horse-racing tracks in the state.

Products & Resources

Ocean Beaches

Sandy beaches and barrier islands stretch for about 130 miles (200 km) along the Atlantic Coast. Two of the state's greatest natural resources are its state parks at Sandy Hook in the north and Island Beach in the south. Visitors enjoy the beaches while the nearby marshes are filled with wildlife.

Cranberries

New Jersey is one of the nation's leading producers of cranberries. The cranberry bogs are located in the northern part of the Interior Coastal Plain. The wetlands there are easily flooded for harvesting the berries. Blueberries and peaches are also major products.

Transportation

New Jersey has one of the busiest, most modern transportation systems in the world. Hundreds of millions of vehicles travel each year on the 148-mile-long (238-km-long) New Jersey Turnpike. Newark Liberty International Airport is one of the busiest airports in the country, and the Port of New York and New Jersey is one of the country's busiest ports.

Satellites

The state's research laboratories have played a key role in developing modern telecommunications. The first satellite used for weather observation was developed in New Jersey in 1960. The first satellite used to beam live pictures between the United States and Europe was also created at a New Jersey research center.

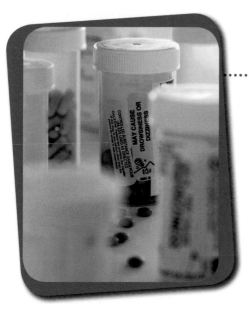

Pharmaceuticals

New Jersey has long been a center for drug research, manufacturing, and sales. Recently, some big drug makers have merged with out-of-state companies. Factories have closed and jobs have been lost. At the same time, many small companies have sprung up that do research in the growing field of biotechnology.

Greenhouses and Nurseries

Products grown in nurseries and greenhouses provide the largest portion of the state's agricultural income. Nurseries produce a wide variety of shrubs, such as juniper and holly. Greenhouses provide New York City markets with roses, geraniums, lilies, orchids, and poinsettias.

Challenging Times

New Jersey—along with the rest of the country—struggled through difficult economic times in the early 1990s. Many people were unemployed, and government studies showed an increase in poverty levels. The economy began to recover in 1993. For the next ten years, New Jersey, and most of the nation, enjoyed prosperity. During this period, the state made great progress in rebuilding its decaying cities, establishing new wildlife areas, and improving existing ones. New nonpolluting industries provided job opportunities. Service industries such as insurance and real estate began to grow.

New Jersey suffered again from a severe economic downturn that began in the United States in late 2007 and grew much worse the next year. By the end of 2009, nearly 10 percent of New Jersey's workforce was unemployed. New Jerseyans were hopeful that the economy would rebound, so that more people would have good jobs.

Balancing the Economy and the Environment

Throughout most of the 1900s, New Jersey's factories produced a wealth of products, but they also created gloomy clouds of smog. Rivers and lakes were polluted with chemicals and waste.

In the last part of the century, the state made progress in cleaning up rivers and streams. Abandoned factories and shipyards were replaced with modern housing and recreation areas. Special attention was also paid to the state's native plants and animals. State lawmakers introduced strict rules regarding pollution and land development.

Private organizations such as the Nature Conservancy and the New Jersey Audubon Society have helped promote policies that save open spaces. In 1978, for example, the Pinelands National Reserve was established to limit development and protect the environment. The reserve covers 1,700 square miles (4,400 sq km) of the Atlantic Coastal Plain. This large area was the country's first national reserve. Much of it is forested land that can be reached only by foot.

Fans flock to the Prudential Center on its opening night 2007. The multimillion-dollar sports and entertainment arena is part of a plan to boost the economy of Newark, the biggest city in the Garden State.

Another bold plan involved the development and protection of the Hackensack Meadows, commonly known as the Meadowlands. This region of marshlands and ponds was created by the last Ice Age. Different agencies manage the land and try to protect native plants and animals and control pollution. The land has also been used to develop a unique area that includes major sports and entertainment facilities. The Meadowlands area is an example of how New Jersey's residents and agencies can work together to protect the land while also finding ways to help the economy.

As New Jersey continues to grow, the effort to balance economic growth with environmental protection will be an ongoing challenge for the Garden State.

State Flag & Seal

*The New Jersey state flag has the official state seal
against a yellow background.*

*The state seal shows two women standing on opposite sides of a shield.
The shield has three plows, which represent agriculture. The woman
to the left of the shield represents liberty. The woman to the right of the
shield represents agriculture. Below the women and the shield are the
words "Liberty and Prosperity" and "1776," the year of independence.*

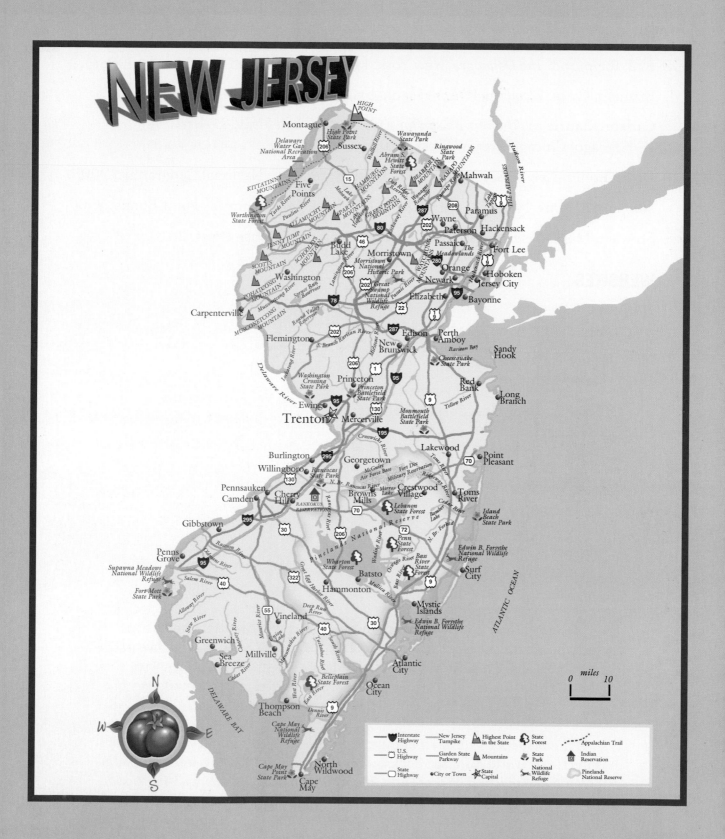

NEW JERSEY

Montague

HIGH POINT

Delaware Water Gap National Recreation Area

High Point State Park

(206) Sussex

Walkill River

Wawayanda State Park

Ringwood State Park

RAMAPO MOUNTAINS

Mahwah

KITTATINNY MOUNTAINS

Five Points

(15)

HAMBURG MOUNTAINS

Abram S. Hewitt State Forest

PEQUANNOCK MOUNTAIN

Lake Mohawk

Oak Ridge Reservoir

Wanaque Reservoir

RAMAPO MOUNTAINS

HUDSON RIVER

Worthington State Forest

Yards Creek River

Pauline River

ALLAMUCHY MOUNTAIN

SPARTA MOUNTAINS

GREEN POND MOUNTAIN

(287)

(208)

Wayne

Paramus

JENNY JUMP MOUNTAIN

SCHOOLEY'S MOUNTAIN

(80)

(202)

Paterson

Hackensack

SCOTTS MOUNTAIN

Budd Lake

(46)

Morristown

WATCHUNG MOUNTAINS

Passaic

The Meadowlands

Fort Lee

POHATCONG MOUNTAIN

Washington

Morristown National Historic Park

(280)

Orange

Hackensack River

Hoboken

Lamington River

(206)

Great Swamp National Wildlife Refuge

Passaic River

Newark

Jersey City

Carpenterville

MUSCONETCONG MOUNTAIN

Spruce Run Reservoir

(202)

(78)

Elizabeth

(95)

Bayonne

Muscanetcong River

Round Valley Reservoir

(22)

(1)

Flemington

(202)

S. Branch Raritan River

(287)

Edison

Perth Amboy

Sandy Hook

Millstone River

New Brunswick

Raritan Bay

DELAWARE RIVER

Lockatong River

Washington Crossing State Park

(1)

Princeton

Princeton Battlefield State Park

(95)

Cheesequake State Park

Red Bank

Long Branch

(9)

Yellow River

(95)

Ewing

Trenton

Mercerville

Monmouth Battlefield State Park

(130)

(195)

Crosswicks River

Lakewood

(70)

Point Pleasant

Burlington

(295)

Georgetown

McGuire Air Force Base

Fort Dix Military Reservation

Toms River

Ridgeway River

Willingboro

Rancocas State Park

(130)

N. Br. Rancocas River

Mirror Lake

Crestwood Village

(72)

Toms River

Pennsauken

Camden

Cherry Hill

RANKOKUS RESERVATION

Browns Mills

(70)

Lebanon State Forest

Bomber Lake

Cedar River

Island Beach State Park

Rancocas River

N. Br. Forest

Gibbstown

(295)

(30)

(206)

Penn State Forest

Bass River State Forest

Edwin B. Forsythe National Wildlife Refuge

Pinelands National Reserve

Oswego River

Bass River

(9)

Surf City

Penns Grove

(95)

Raccoon River

Great Egg Harbor River

Wharton State Forest

Batsto

Mullica River

Mystic Islands

Supawna Meadows National Wildlife Refuge

Salem River

(322)

ATLANTIC OCEAN

Fort Mott State Park

Alloway River

(40)

Hammonton

(30)

Edwin B. Forsythe National Wildlife Refuge

Stow River

(55)

Deep Run River

Maurice River

(40)

Atlantic City

Greenwich

Union Lake

Menantico River

South River

Tuckahoe River

Sea Breeze

Millville

Cohansey River

Cedar River

West River

Belleplain State Forest

East River

Ocean City

DELAWARE BAY

Thompson Beach

Dennis River

(9)

Cape May National Wildlife Refuge

North Wildwood

Cape May Point State Park

Cape May

Compass rose showing N, S, E, W

Legend

Interstate Highway	New Jersey Turnpike	Highest Point in the State	State Forest	Appalachian Trail
U.S. Highway	Garden State Parkway	Mountains	State Park	Indian Reservation
State Highway	City or Town	State Capital	National Wildlife Refuge	Pinelands National Reserve

miles
0   10

MORE ABOUT NEW JERSEY

BOOKS

Bial, Raymond. *The Delaware*. New York: Marshall Cavendish Benchmark, 2005.

Brunelli, Carol. *Woodrow Wilson*. Mankato, MN: The Child's World, 2009.

Carlson, Laurie M. *Thomas Edison for Kids, His Life and Ideas, 21 Activities*. Chicago: Chicago Review Press, 2006.

Doak, Robin. *New Jersey, 1609–1776*. Washington, DC: National Geographic, 2005.

Nobleman, Marc Tyler, *The Hindenburg*. Mankato, MN: Compass Point Books, 2006.

Stewart, Mark. *New Jersey Devils*. Chicago: Norwood House Press, 2010.

WEBSITES

Hangout NJ:
http://www.state.nj.us/hangout_nj

New Jersey Tourism:
http://www.visitnj.org

The Official State of New Jersey Website:
http://www.nj.gov

David C. King is an award-winning author who has written more than forty books for children and young adults. He and his wife, Sharon, live in the Berkshires at the junction of New York, Massachusetts, and Connecticut. Their travels have taken them through most of the United States. New Jersey has always been one of their favorite states to visit.

William McGeveran is a longtime reference book editor and was editorial director at World Almanac Books, where he managed the development of *The World Almanac and Book of Facts*, *The World Almanac for Kids*, and *The World Almanac Book of Records*. Now a freelance writer and an editor, he has written and edited articles on current events and other topics for an online encyclopedia and other reference works. Bill and his wife have four grown children.

78

Page numbers in **boldface** are illustrations.